Along the Road from Eden

For Bill and Nancy
Many thanks for all
your kindness.

George Elliboloy
Lethbridge
Nov 1990

Along
the Road
from Eden

George
Ellenbogen

SIGNAL
EDITIONS

SIGNAL EDITIONS IS AN IMPRINT OF VEHICULE PRESS MONTREAL CANADA

I would like to acknowledge with thanks the encouragement of my editor, Michael Harris; the blessed competence of my publisher, Simon Dardick; the many helpful insights of Evelyn Shakir; the careful proofreading of Cheryl Rendel, Joan Oliveri, Mary Jellis, and Diane Viveiros; and the time and resources given to me by Bentley College, the Michael Karolyi Foundation, the Montalvo Association, and the Virginia Center for the Creative Arts.

Some of these poems have appeared in the following periodicals and anthologies:
Partisan Review, New Boston Review, Revue Europe, Poetry Australia, Literary Review, Boston Today, Nantucket Review, Arc, Blue Unicorn, Canadian Forum, Dalhousie Review, Descant, Kansas Quarterly, Matrix, The Echo Room, Amelia, California State Poetry Quarterly, Canadian Author and Bookman, Waves, Epos, Anthology of Magazine Verse and Year Book of American Poetry 1980, Anthology of Magazine Verse and Year Book of American Poetry 1981, Traductière, Essential Words: An Anthology of Jewish Canadian Poetry and *The Father's Book: Shared Experiences*.

Published with the assistance of the Canada Council
Series editor: Michael Harris
Cover design by JW Stewart
Photograph of the author by Geneviève Stephenson
Typeset in Garamond by Zibra Inc.
Printed by Les Éditions Marquis Ltée.

Ellenbogen, George, 1934-
    Along the road from Eden
ISBN 0-919890-94-6
    I. Title.
PS8559.L542A46 1989   C811'.54   C89-090140-6
PR9199.3.E44A46 1989

Véhicule Press, P.O.B. 125, Place du Parc Station,
Montreal, Quebec   Canada   H2W 2M9

Printed in Canada.

It is to my parents, Moses and the late Jennie Ellenbogen,
and my children, Sara Ellenbogen Ekonomakis and Adam,
that I dedicate these poems.

CONTENTS

IN THE CLOSE OF DARKNESS

THE WAY WE SANG

VIEWS AND RECOLLECTIONS

SAFARI—NIGHTFALL

You stake out one more Monday as you turn
your sweaty back in morning heat that hangs
like morning breath, an egg your waking tongue
administers until the edges burn
with indifference. Marriage, affairs, flip
like atlas pages in our listless hands
as we pad in slippers light years from bends
we descend towards, an earlier kinship
where blood sun plummets into sand,
spreads orange ears on eucalyptus leaves,
white pores open on the waves; by a strand
Thompson gazelles dart out like fireflies,
one into a slump of lions; a lone jacana
descends upon the dark savannah.

DELPHI

Like hawk and sparrow we descend, the dish
is travel. After all, it's May. The corn
will come. And reassured we leave
Syntagma's coffee cups for Thebes
and Delphi, slipping into pilgrimage.

From villages raised around flokatis
and burros posing for pictures
the bus, pausing back
to first gear, climbs
like a lame pilgrim into creams
of lower clouds.

    From Pergamum and the Euphrates they
came with boxes of mysteries inlaid
in lapis lazuli, and trudged
through heat and hawkers of smoked fish,
one legged beggars
supplementing a pension
for what the traffic would bear.
Stillness squatted around the temple like stone
lions, and they lay down their treasure — pithoi
marked "Marathon," "Salamis,"
"Plataea," all treasured days.

By crowds brandishing
Baedekers we flow
into gullies;
the temple of Zeus
is empty —
           Were they like us,
        gawkers on a tourist bus? —

                    a few last blades
of grass sprout from caked soil.
It is Tuesday, the museum closed, the
charioteer alone; no feet at the starting
post, no theatric declamation.
The road below stretches
into stands of limonada and coke.

What is happening in the Tholos?
Who is being sent
to lead an army
or unravel a riddle?

At Syntagma former sailors
(they are all former sailors
with brothers where you live)
invite you to their bars
to rooster your love away.

The gulls have stop circling
the shore; boulders are falling on the road;
the mountains breathing up their stones,
and the oracles blind and unheard.

NEW HOUSES/OLD HOUSES

Ultimately
they cannot
hold a death
being already dead.

Stalled they sit-
uate one hundred feet apart,
sealed by sac-crete
and a picture tube.

Nothing juts out
in bays of neo-gothic craze,
nothing violates
the supremacy of the box.

What happens
on the wall-
to-wall rugs, what
bodies rub and sink
lump snuggled into polyethylene
softness?

The houses we remember—
there are always houses
        we remember—
have become Holiday Inns,
and the clothed naked have dropped
from old valleyed beds
into an olympic swimming pool.

It sets upon me now,
the suburban peace
with hospitals,
with soft soled shoes
in endless corridors,
where death is made respectable
and becomes its own hotel.

PENNSYLVANIA DUTCH

Shop upon shop
each settled with kitsch
squats in the flatness
along three-four-o.

Splicing the horizon
windmills spin over
green miniature squares,
yellow cubes of hay.

Token Amish prod ahead
hoof by lumbering hoof. Swarms
of kodak click pursuit.
Entombed in black traps,

a piltdown joke, a prey
tour guides noise around,
they till and hide
from the light of their countryside;

then hesitate through Sunday
troubled by passing cars,
by the maniacal rush of blood,
the flow in electrical veins

where Blue
Ball follows
Intercourse and all
dancing sex
teases
under scripture.

THEY DON'T MAKE DEPRESSIONS THE WAY THEY USED TO

with people
dropping
out of skies

and all mornings
all tumbling
into long lines of neighbors
huddling
for heat
on raw days.

They don't.
Not the way
they used to make them.
No one walks
out of the valley
of his dying skull
into the Gulf of Mexico.

We hear it all;
we always hear.
All on the news
we hear. We
are shut in, our
antennae made by Zenith,
our comfort by Ritz
on plastic trays. We
forget on crackers.

Even our depressions
have grown corns
and turned to prose.

Even the sun seems to pause
between camel back clouds
noting the occasion, Sunday
on the Square. Each neighboring street
decants the crowds, presents accents
from Cyprus, the Indies, emerging
shiekdoms. Their voices surround
monument after monument; pigeons
come to every calling hand. Their feathers
blur the stones of South Africa House.
In a lower corner squats Canada
House, colonial gray, obsequious below
the gray rise of the National Gallery.
Behind, in exile, portraits of Jonson and More,
bold icons both, stare out in shadow.
The lions, now tame, lie down with lambs
who scale their loins while parents photograph.
The Nelson Column still survives,
a maypole folk dance around.
Check the records. This is how it happens,
how it has always happened.
While sun edges the colonnade
of St. Martin-in-the-Fields,
two vergers flap among the pious
selling orange squash for God.

TOWARDS NINEVEH

The road winds
like loose wool
turned by paws
on green carpet.

Things in the distance squat—
tents perhaps—
preen themselves in desert twilight,
stare with lanterned eyes.

Horse offal turns dark
before darkness
as the heavens tent out
over the sand.

We shall soon
descend to Nineveh
camel by camel
and watch the flames
go out
on the last adulteries.

THE DRIFTING

It had, he laughed, to happen just that way:
the Church rising out of chicken soup
and Christ, like Aphrodite, a discard
was a restaurant joke we knew would play

to the kids on the street; so we played
it after *cheder* like the rubber ball
we bounced till dark off the lumber yard wall
(that stands even now through sun and rage).

Not that we always chose to stay.
We drifted to tag, to bleeding air
from tires, to local laughter
at the fierce-bearded Moses

who filled a window judging down
as we, growing to games of hand in hand,
strutted below in ties and danced
against the trembling of the gowns.

We pause now by splintered stairs
raising ghosts by anecdote until
our conjurings, borne by splintered voice,
emerge from corners into view again.

What can I say about this corner shop
where once old men with talliths streamed
through starred doors, crazed with song and prayer
now staged for shelves of towelling and pop?

We linger, scuffing around old sites,
finding only the strange in what is left.
As rain blurred the lumber sign, we knew
the ball was gone, and we were all bereft.

BARON BYNG HIGH — A REVISIT

It is fall. Two

grey squirrels
thrash through the leaves,
throwing them and all
memories into chaos

as I step over thresholds
onto square after square
avoiding
                          the lines, listening
as steps on squares from the end
of corridors grow and grow
and soften into muffle, leaving
faces that hang for twenty years —
nameless portraits I carry, hold
close
        and duck as two children
tearing round a corner
throw imaginary balls at my head
behind the window pane.

Whatever balls bounced
against those schoolyard walls
bounced our names and sang
a call to last
as long as the pock of tennis balls.

The rooms become like one another.
Bells arrest the afternoon; faces
turned, the hands assembling books
are not the hands and faces I
measured by. Four students make their way
out. I, alone, follow.

Lines drifting
parallel behind me
recall the day and leaves;
all things scraping gutters
settle against their private stone.
In empty corridors I hear those names—
Jerry Burke, Evelyn Petrushka—
who ran so lightly over stone,
tiptoed over the binomial theorem
and laid all declension to rest.

FAMILY COUNSELING

No one they tell me really comes through.
They walk out the way they arrive,
perhaps a half step slower, a sigh
yielding a softer scream. Samburu
limps to mind: the press and flight
across the plain, the last bound to
the carcass slipping blood, the wound
just ripe, eyes slanting left and right.
They go to it—like lovers exploring,
wedging the widened opening; worry
flesh until surprises of bone wall free
and snarls leap out to thin the gathering;
dropping into a last stretch they creep
to shade, licking their chops, and pause for sleep.

THE END OF THE AFFAIR

We arrange the Meissen between us
(tundish for you, tureen pushed to my side),
dividing the final rags of a marriage
from an affair several years dead.

Our hands shepherd transparencies
one by one to light to view
until birthdays and vacations fall
like sheared fleece upon the hardwood floor.

The books fall more readily
into rank, soldiering stiffly
for what we used at night
to keep from one another's sight.

And records—call them music
if you will—we add contempt
to each release. A hurried trade
speeds some last knick-knacks on their way.

And two more, aged twelve and eight,
we consign to weekends, holidays;
ourselves to minutes parked in driveways
watching parentage slip away.

The bed, old scarred four-poster,
hides like an embarrassment upstairs
because after many turns and twistings
it will not squeeze through the bedroom door.

THE HITCHHIKER

She was all that was left
after the sudden shower
with the dust held down,
the meadows packed with rain.

She brought to us few words,
a pack that remained
for one day, then two,
finally a week, and eyes
that haunted the edge of our fire.

We reassemble her
in Christmas cards,
wedding announcement,
picture of a child
humped in a blanket
at one year old.

She remains with us now
like weather and kitchens,
ranges we accustom to,
as we wait for her
to follow her last letter
through the front door.

ELEGY FOR A CHILD WHO FELL

This fallen child, whose empty eyes
poems could not harmonize,
nor the reaching requiem
contain the wood enclosing him

slips from the circled reach of eyes
without a jolt, without surprise,
whose stuttered step has stumbled in
to words that now embroider him.

FOR ELLA WHO DIED

The word is that she was jarred
across Kansas in a covered wagon
and hunched in the darkest corner
of the cellar when a cyclone
drove the barn to the next county
and her east, city by temporary
city, garden by garden on the way,

a sentence she carried like a ring
for years. She laid her weight against
an oaken board, presiding over daily
coffee, nightly talk and whiskey,
the drift of wobblies, new boarders
who always came at night to spring
rumpled scarves and visions for the world.

She loved kids and, often, love,
had enough left over even in winter
for the cowbird, for the mourning dove,
the stretch of table at Thanksgiving
as she governed family, food and drink;
the procession of plate and glass
to waterfalls in the kitchen sink.

Across the narrow throat of street
she stared on winter afternoons
checking it all: the crest of waxwing
cruising its space for crumbs she spread;
granted the seasons their wandering
weather, would rake the remnants,
and flowers grew in her dominion.

Is it because of this, her tending
through years of garden that I forgive
the years of lumbering across our lives,
the voice and stare we never crossed
although her aging step allowed escape?
To the very end she turned her spade
in flower beds to house our mortgaged lives.

So I long for there to be clean stone
severely arranged, no wandered weed
splitting the line with reaching stem—
a too long snake of truth. Let it lie
here where sparrows and cardinals twist
from one another, leaves turn in
their time, and gardeners never rest.

THE WORSHIPPERS OF BEATRICE

I sense the faces of these breathing souls
that carry in the wind at Montaillou
who worshipped Beatrice de Planisoles.

While Othon slept, Pierre Clergue was heard to roll
with Beatrice between the casks of brew.
I sense the faces of these breathing souls.

Medallions of Chatelain Roquefort show
a lover dead before his wisdom grew.
He worshipped Beatrice de Planisoles.

By aging breasts Aurilhac the zealot stole
those secrets of Cathar her passion drew.
I sense the faces of these breathing souls.

The yellow cross, her heretic's parole,
pursued her more than all those lovers knew
who worshipped Beatrice de Planisoles.

Recall her in the passes to Querol,
who trembled thighs in spite of Fournier's crew.
I sense the faces of these breathing souls
who worshipped Beatrice de Planisoles.

While married to Othon de Lagleize, Beatrice committed adultery with the priest,
Pierre Clergue
•
Beranger de Rocquefort, Beatrice's first husband, died young
•
Barthelemy Aurilhac threatened to expose Beatrice's Cathar heresies
•
Condemned heretics were required to wear crosses of yellow material on the backs of their
outer garments.
•
Querol was a summer settlement of the Cathars
•
Jacques Fournier, inquisitor at Pamier, later became Pope Benedict XII in Avignon

AFTER THE SPECTACLE

I knew
Manute Bol
whose thighs
no wider than his ankles
stretched
in mid air beside
a ball bouncing
beyond where gossip leaps
and trophies line a wall.

The smile opened round
two stray teeth declares
he is like us — brushes
his teeth, both of them,
does exercises in agreement
and puzzles over the binomial theorem
his head tilted like fruit
over a lined sheet

except when unaware
of Gulliver he curls back
in the babyhood of his Austin
(instead of carrying it)
and admits remainders and fractions
to the whole numbers
trailing his equations.

But these are desert pauses
where camels squat
and words become grains
of sand far
from today's
business

        where a small sad head
presides
far from the Sudan
in a land
of baskets and boards
that no one visits
for very long.

29

OUTSIDE IERAPETRA

> "It is from here that everything
> can come. It is from here that
> everything begins."
> André Breton, *Nadja*

A hard place in season
where no plant now flourishes,
stubble nibbled to rock
by daily passage of goats.

Still the place in season screams
with lust. Sun bakes the ground.
The ground resounds with shepherd step.
In silence, heat lifts from stone,
screams its high pitch out to sea.

In black shawls, two women bear
lemons. Local tales announce the taste
for blood, sacrifice, and procession.
I pass all this with camera and book;
gringo and exile, I stoop and peer

and know—I suddenly know
as the last man on the platform
knows the last train has gone
that a beginning is here, in this
rugged outcrop, a heavy breath

heaved what cradles me now;
those black shawled women, herdsmen,
and goats—this is fossil harbor
where shapes of energy twist in stone
and lie impressed in Phaestos and Zakros.

Laboring separately
we are arranged as a montage
for tomorrow's history class
until sun drops below the ruins
and we drop from mountain slopes
into selves that encrust in the dark.

A LETTER FROM IERAPETRA

The sun has baked the ground
for seven days. The goats
denude the slope. Some scrub
remains, some blades of grass.
I blow cigar smoke
at the sun, stoke sand into pools
with my toes.

It is half a creation ago. Remains
of a wall set by the sea —
a fortress (each island town
has one or invents one).

A figure halfway up the hill
nurses earth around young vines.
Body hunched, he never doubts
the May appearance of the grape.
Many miles away
another figure hunched
reassembles shards
craning towards an image
buried for thousands of years.

In the north the oracles say
the earth will perish under ice.
The boats have seeped from the sea,
the sun has dried the wind,
and the swell stilled to glass.

I will return in June
when I hear nothing under my feet
but the sound of pebble on pebble
with a pot of gardenias
under each arm.

ICONS AND VOICES

THE DIVER

Shifted downwind by the tide
he slopes to stabilize himself,
slants his shoulders down to see
what tidal shove has spread beneath:
hints of coral, spider crabs,
fractured shells, anemone,
caught, like him, in ocean roll.

With hosed nose and wishful gills
a transient returns to probe
the solemn rites that distance him;

then to right himself turns
fins to catch the amniotic push
and lets its fluid encircle him.

THE ESSENTIAL HARDNESS

It followed a lingering drunk
that morning — late one at that,
and spotted in the yard were pools
of frost that gripped the garden fast.

At least so they turned out to be
when we approached as if to confirm
what always turns out to be a death
though the frost around was not so firm.

Some parsley, for instance, still reached
for sun, a fern too, but we knew
by wind it was much beyond Eden,
picked a sprig or two, resigned the rest.

That essential hardness we saw through glass
is no more than the anchor we know inside
that roots us to our seasonal watch
against the seasonal claims we hatch.

Still, when snow overwhelms those spots,
we forget the promises once called in
and linger in memories springs have warmed,
pressing fallen blossoms against bare skin.

BELOW THE FAIREST FRUIT

Between the cesspool and the sink
the flowers of Arcadia grow;
the blossoms tilting at the sun
obscure the ironwork below.

The axe that falls on Trotsky's head
dissidents finally understand
forms technocrats' dachas by the sea,
their amorous windings on the sand.

By the cyrillics of the monuments
worshippers nod at what they glean;
state gardeners in dry weather hose
the crippled grass to keep it green.

BEFORE THE MARINER

Like the mariner we all confess again
in littered streets where children store their shouts
through hide and seek. Their silence stretches out
an afternoon. No corpse, no squeal of pain;
our guilt lighter than an albatross,
the albatross lighter than a rain
that stretches down the rust of copper drain
pipe. Stretches like beach front that we cross
teasing grains of sand till tide swells spray
crusts of salt that weigh on dancing feet
or surround love winding like a place
to return to, a spider crab's splayed
shell splintering arguments to send
us out for albatross with bow in hand.

THE REVISIT

The old two-deck houses retain
me little more than John who nods,
weighs a mound of figs and adds
"How's the wife," three years gone,
dried away from me, my current
one hand grasp away, a train I always
miss. I mumble something only
mandarins understand and John
is no mandarin.

My kids collect some oranges and change,
struggle through drifts of snow searching
out old sites that hide but reemerge
like old toys: a half covered sign, Stone's Drugs,
calming as sleep, turns us round a corner;
the pizzeria venting parmesan
through lips of ice around a wire mouth,
its clapboard shingle chapped to green flakes.

Soldiering through a haze of hidden bulbs,
salt sticks and muffins barricade a shelf,
below the pumpernickels all in disarray.
Next door an auto parts store going broke,
some scattered spark plugs and a sign—
a reclining body on a bed of sand
smiling to sell a bar of soap—nothing
more but loops of wire and a length of rope,

mysteries that couple me like a shape
of winter breath puffing in pilgrimage
after old tracks, old traces, and old words.
We follow slopes down streets, a reminiscence
we ran down twenty years ago, craning eye
and ear for what we neither see nor hear;
in this discovered darkness all alone
we plod like dogs, sniffing from tree to tree.

There are no moons like those we used to know
that shone the way whenever the power failed,
or so we claim, as we haul our shopping bags
and pass like fugitives to the family car
(some remnants of body heat still remain).
Grudging, we cruise by the lighted doorways
and squinting find that all the names have gone
well beyond appeal and will not be caught.

CIRCUIT

Several things I suppose
make me aware of it: the priest
outside Nikos' taverna, closed
for no apparent reason, the cover
of *Farewell to Arms* randomly open.
Nothing works out; the bridge
always collapses.

Two days of wind have blown away
the almond blossoms; even Angelos'
window blown away, his icons
scattered on the floor; summer
affairs beached like bathers
collapsed on sand.

The dancers here rarely dance,
are out of step, stumble against
the music; dogs in midday heat yelp,
stuck in one another.

              As you sleep
I am aware you are now
as far as stars I sit under.
A dog howls again and again,
the cicadas break into a chatter
that does not break; the bells
of sheep pursue
two fireflies darting
round a post.
A donkey's bray breaks the spell.
The symphony is accidental, each
part a turn around a post
that makes no sense
by the lamp that gives it light.

The nets have been folded, last
boats nudge into port, lamps
dim out.

                                   Over my ouzo I see
the shimmering lights of Scotaros
but they are distant
and do not provide.

MOURNING

Nothing for most of the day would tell you,
even if you looked closely, for instance, like
stepping off a bus to study pictures
on a wall that gave clues of shade or stroke
that she buried her husband this June.

Settling her days like great plains, she
buttons a tunic over two layers
of clothes and flosses her teeth
to soap operas between two and three,
but never steps beyond the hedge for mail.

So the car sits like a prehistoric site;
her navigation is from room to room,
rearranging lives on the telephone,
spreading crumbs for a bullfinch and *mes anges*,
poking corners each Monday with a broom.

Before you smirk, think of the rotted stump
that unsettles us each year at winter thaw
and how we walk a hundred ways to miss
the snow's release of its disfigured wood
that living temperatures torture into view.

GRADUATION OF THE SECONDARY SCHOOL CLASSICAL STUDENTS IN ROTTERDAM

It may have been here
that two tonners
obliterated the days
and made Rotterdam
a lunar landscape, here
where afternoon light slants
on concrete and parents
slant to the rector's summary:
>   "Henrik was weak
>   in math, but improved, and Mauritz
>   distinguished himself in Greek..."
here
where the Waffen's trucks
skimmed the flatlands like snipes
swallowing flies,
their hands rooting out workers
like turnips
for the plant at Arnhem.

                    There
fathers hid in chests, became
part of the indoor
brickwork (unacknowledged
portraiture),
made, finally, for the cities
and became
part of a gray human drift
that remained.

Here
this other site once
was scooped out like egg yolk
with shell splinters of skull
and brick and earth and old
beginnings.

It goes on.
Buildings go up and weeds
grow into crotched corners
of walls — no matter what, it
all happens again;
and these students
who have scanned Pindar's *Odes* and
the *Ars Amatoria*
shake several hands and sign
their names to an opening door
walking each in his turn
to what accident has trimmed
and teachers cannot withhold.

THE EQUIVOCATOR

We knew him as an end
of tables we sat around
and yawned towards.
Neither for nor against
nor neutral, he spoke,
made nevertheless a law
and clarity a joke. He
could be counted on every issue
to guide syllable after syllable
into long darkened trains
of lost ends and forgotten beginnings.

Conviction
vibrating in his hands, he pressed
on the injustice of the rising, any
rising, leaning this way
and sometimes that,
navigating between certainties
as solidity became mines
he shifted between.

We watched and knew
he would excel in lathers of shampoo,
vanishing into pancake mix
or floating into commas,
emerging at daybreak —
an exhausted phoenix —
as weak cereal
and murmuring syntax.

QUESTIONS OF PULSE

Our drumsticks beating on the drum
are measured sound, old thumping pulse;
the mouse exploring what it smells
will find its circles always round.

What Madame's ocelot digests
it swallows with Decembered roar,
its jungle pounce forgotten now
for scratchings on a hardwood floor.

Flying saucers under stars,
swaths across the Nazca plain
equate beyond our wall to wall;
we pare and cancel; we

who walk a measured pace
squint at birdflight to the sun,
rejoicing at dismembered cults
to drumsticks beating on a drum.

BERMUDA TRIANGLE

The water under sky turned gray
and weight descended on his watch.
Weight held the hands, tuckered time,
perplexed all gulls, and flying fish
dispersed and emptied out the sky.

Five Avengers tipped their wings
droning in the sinking air;
three men blinking in each plane
with nothing to avenge or watch
as wave reached after falling wave
into swells of ocean thud.

Ceilings of cloud pressed down in
sky that darkened without rain
under sun that wrinkled gray.
Insanity trembled in the wings,
the nose bent towards the drawing sea
despite the wrenching of the wheel.

Busy fingers feathered past
buttons that merely disobeyed.
Radio messages leapt out
seeking familiar complements,
sets of familiar latitudes.
"Give me your bearings," came back,
like a fireman on a phone
exhorting children in a fire
to recite the ABC.

No one saw five spinning planes
though numbers offered to explain
the strange and awkward plummetings,
like acrobats dropping into space
as ripple vaulted over ripple
landscaping our ocean fears.

Haunted homes are what we crave,
apocrypha moving from room to room,
so that we never understand
or reason at the window pane,
content to count our freedom in
old gropings in the living room.

Yet on days with equal light
we consult our manuals
and alter seascapes into graphs
until the hemisphere becomes
a familiar picnic ground
where kites unwind from children's hands
while gray and body sucking waves
tack like tinder in the mind.

HIS WAY

His was a step we always knew; his stare
declared a path clear from his parking space
to desks he presided over, a deep chair
he overlapped, musing, puffing away
at each typist's morning flurry, always
teasing the ticking clock, that nothing
was worth running for; and so he never ran

except on late afternoons when he moved
into a half trot to pencilled books
he bordered with his hands, approved
strips of phrase, spare worlds he took
with him. And when he swelled his nook
with laughter, so enchanted his beer,
a glass of Bud, he made it disappear.

In slanting sunlight he governed his rows
of earth against the spread of weed,
the fury of dandelions into yellow.
He cared when his glories were not freed
to bloom, nor favorite sagas there to read;
tendered himself as page to those he tended
like Gilmore Sims and others he'd befriended.

And so we wish him cakes and ale
that bristles in afternoon stillness,
pages that quicken the waiting line,
a settling calm to settle fast
by edging shadows on the grass
which we know as his way
of having dinner with the world.

IN THE CLOSE OF DARKNESS

THE RENEWAL

We are coming to it again.
Again they are in the streets
scrawling on the walls.

Who is the victim now?
For whom are the fires lit?
Whom will the burning save?

Why the knock on the door?
What paper must I sign
to liberate myself?

Books are heaved on the flames,
reduced to cinder and ash
as howls swell through the night.

The readers are hauled out again,
made to parade on the square
with placards announcing their crimes.

In silence we sit at our desks,
neighbors removed each day.
No one raises his head.

No one begins to ask why;
the streets are silent now.
New faces sit at the desks.

I listen to my feet
tap along empty streets
past the occasional guard,

imagine myself uncoiled
in the scents of the Sporades
under the stunted pines.

The floor beneath the trees
is soft, a needle bed
cushions me under the moon.

Inside old stone huts
lovers in whispers
unfold throughout the night.

I watch my hand reach out
to a woman I must have known
beside me in the grove.

There is only silence now;
the tavernas have all closed down.
The guards are standing at call.

I reach out to that woman
beside me in the grove
and find she has turned to stone.

SOME RECOLLECTIONS OF THE LAST ORT CLASSES
IN THE WARSAW GHETTO

While we solved for x
in the ORT algebra class
with the prescribed scholarly hunch
in desks neatly arranged
by masters who had sat
in desks neatly arranged,
others with yellow stars
sewn on tattered coats
moved through the shadow of walls
from the thud of distant boots.

Whatever collapsed in the street,
we knew on the hour of nine
electrical current ran
humming its geometry
into equations until
the landscapes that we saw
burned through window panes
were bodies in the wind
kept by telegraph poles
and Ohm's Law collapsed
and the movement of the stars.

The alleys shrank to a slit
through which we slipped to class,
the rubble in the street we knew
at last were corpses piled
that thwarted every step.
Logarithms became
the music of their death.

We knew it was ended
when boots kicked us over,
hands heaped us onto carts,
and even the ORT class
had rung out for the year.

THE INVASION

They did not clank. We would have heard
the clank of tanks treading through grey
underlips of streets to empty squares.

We would have seen the crowds, the chase
sputtering leaflets, raised clubs ending
like a dirge in littered doorways.

Perhaps we dreamed the empty rings
of roads, the tap of a last passerby
disappearing through doors, emerging

in conspiracies of two which multiply
like me and you in window seats
swelling like an emptiness of sky.

Next day the ceremony repeats,
motion funneling into cards
that identify all births, all needs;

the scar of check lists, the arched
eyebrow, pen stroke and expected shove
into waiting vans. The parks

are cleaner now; sweepers in droves
broom away apple cores that bone
through concrete walks, remove

most traces. Posters are new. Zone
stripes now are green. Geraniums bloom. Eine
Kleine Nachtmusik spins off the gramophone.

But the nights are long, the frost binds
like a prison on the panes. Phones remain
like props, the words choked on the lines.

In the metro, swirls of graffiti stain
the whitewashed walls. Violins scratch
chords across the departing roar of trains.

Thunder cracks across the piercing wedge
of planes; they bend in unison. A cleft
of lightning zigs anarchically. We watch

curls of smoke. Flames lift,
tilt from wind through the night.
At dawn only coughs are left.

And the faucet drop by drop
waters an anger in the brain.

DACHAU

Dachau. June 1978

A bus deposits me
in a place I have always known,
my melancholy treasure,
packaged now in silence,
only the dried floral wreathes
rustle in the wind.

Poland. September 1939

That word *milchumah*,
there could be none other,
passed like the angel of death
over the *shtetlach* and fields.
They ran from the Stukas' wings
among mounded stacks of hay,
spooned their terror out
in tablespoons of borscht,
doling rumors out.
The dishes were put away.
No one came by to say
they were the dishes now;
they would have to be smashed
to complete a system or scene.

No one daubed the lintels.

Tanks soon nosed around
the corner where we heard
talmudic conundrums
refined week after week.
Now in a panic of minutes
the walls all came apart;
the officer corps installed
in the homes of the priest and mayor,
new posters appeared on the square.
The rabbi has lost his seat,
is herded along with us.
Some are sealed in trucks,
some pushed onto trains,
the hesitant prodded with butts.
There are faces behind those guns,
lips tense with rage, ears beyond human speech.

Munich. June 1978

I sip alone in a rathskeller
under a Munich street;
Oktoberfest songs
barrel across the room.

Transit 1940 / 1978

In the shadow of the barbed wire fence
while the Blue Danube played,
an engineer and his wife
danced the whole night through
and a train knifed toward Dachau
with another load of Jews.
With friends they watched the dawn
over *Kaffee mit Sahne* and toast,
but the toast was burned, and the Jews
didn't do well either, he said
some years after the war.

58

That chimney still pouts in air,
stout, so fiercely erect,
it could have been fashioned for love.
The records were balanced each day —
arrivals and dispositions :
some charged with malaria,
others sliced open for view,
most thinned from life and fed
to the chimney's genitals,
fed to the oven's desire.

My brain is exploding,
the pieces turn to ask,
the pieces turn to ash
floating up the chimney.
Talmudic phrases scatter
like butterflies in a breeze.
I clutch the barbed wire fence,
wound myself to turn
private grief to public rage —
they had no children. I do not forgive,
I forget, says Camus. But those pictures,
the chimney hungering there,
the heaps of arms and legs,
I see them every time
I turn an atlas page
or a Volkswagon wheel.
I am taught by Yglesias again
whether in pleasure or pain
we stand in the shadow and light
around our father's house.

◆

Lesbos, March 1978

They are dropped by the 2:30 bus
on the stones of Molivos;
with packs they climb the slope,
a group of Bavarians.
Some pause to help an old man
struggling under a load,
others do not pause.
They are young and blond —
my nightmares for thirty years —
but as they pass me by,
there is no blood on the ground,
no corpses under their boots.
Beyond a grief of years
stiffened towards rhetoric
I know these were the children.

Munich. July 1978

The Munich train slips in,
my foot nudges baggage
somewhat lighter now.
Marianne touches me. I see
only the gray in her hair. We
endure another farewell
with the train's outward lurch
toward German countryside.
And yes, I say
to myself, la guerre
est fini, la guerre
est bien fini.

THE EMERGENCE

It was the eighth day or ninth
after the tanks rolled through
and we queued in passport lines

that the frost came in early June
when daffodils had just announced
themselves through cobblestones by ruins

at the exit gate. Days are wounds
we horde like pats of oleo to spread
in growing silence under frowns.

Footsteps cozy up to rumors, fed
by oranges, the gate opening again,
shafts of sunlight; evening spreads

on a human caterpillar chain
growing until the fruit runs out
and it unravels like a spastic brain.

Shop windows all darkened when we scout
for coal. Neighboring windows reveal
nothing behind drawn blinds, nothing wrought

but lines we draw across each meal,
eyes that never rise to fork a mate.
The phone lines have gone dead. We seal

our boredom on unwashed dinner plates,
the bed unmade, the detested furniture,
porcelain bric-a-brac that grates;

still we remember the family pictures
by the lake, plum pits thrown in,
feeling you breathe all night, the elixir

of your breasts like plums on my skin
when swallows coaxed the blinds up at dawn
and you awoke by parts to skim

my thigh; like a mist we rose from
morning; unrolled bolts of light, we grow
into the warming of a battering sun

to hear street chatter by open windows
sunlight storming through the opening gate
and watch through the thinning shadow

slicing out its final wedge of night
and children's laughter curling like a rose.

THE SENTENCE

We're what the Duke of Norfolk knew —
flies ranging round a glass of port —
of exile and an exile's view.

An unstringed viol, a flattish brew,
Plantagenets in every court
were what the Duke of Norfolk knew.

A tongue portcullised to renew
its grunt and spittle, nothing short
of exile and an exile's view.

Horses daily presenting noon,
declensions of Arabic sport,
were what the Duke of Norfolk knew.

A spectator when rumors grew
to war, repeal, his own report
of exile and an exile's view.

The wind's muttered aphasic spew
the sun spinning off the earth
were what the Duke of Norfolk knew
of exile and an exile's view.

THE ALIEN

When ice crusted stone, he arranged
the landscape into words until
even the deaf witnessed birds
singing, careening in cadenced flight
round his measured plots of beech
although ice still attached to sills,
cracked and still encrusted stone,
swelling through the campus yard.

On still snowcovered days sweat comes,
comes now to his face, his tongue numb.
Perhaps it is falling plaster, the world
in need of nails, essays that lumber
like oxen with the same subject questions
falling one step, always one step behind
in a space no one visits. He sat
and stared at windows no birds passed.

It happens. Winter settles too
on more than stone, and snows
are like the snows we wait upon
and sit inside; and all the plots
and measured lawns are indications
that remove; slow drifts swallowed words
he held, and what remained stuttered
in his mouth like loose change
until sound ground to a stop,
his tongue pedalled air,
and silence secured him.

Now he sits beggaring the sun,
accommodating an empty chair,
where patients walk backwards
and play therapeutic golf
on a course without holes,
and even mosquitoes nudge through screens,
making noises that rhyme
in the wrong places.

A hesitant step is all that remains
of seasons, language, while the sun
hibernates in the pockets of his trousers,
and habit lies carelessly along the ground
like scuffed through mounds on gravel paths.

Give him sun and words to turn
stone to soil and greener dreams,
arms of plants to graze his arms,
some flowered face to window to,
new woods to touch his hands
and real hands to grasp them to.

THE CATATONIC TYPIST

No one knew nor did we bother with
the girl we hired to type our scribbled words.
The clack, we thought at first, was all there was
until mistakes and mutters and fierce eyes
made her a ticking in our metronome.

She walked like a taut leopard
stalking the afternoon; her heels
tapped out her message on the floor,
eyes withdrew and catatonic set,
desks on each side turned to walls
as she stepped through her created corridor.

No one knew what held those tight closed lips
although some guessed, silent and privately.
Those eyes staring beyond us into space
we knew were faceless and would turn to stone.

Perhaps she felt the walls, despised the guards
who shifted leg on leg and dumped out words,
handing her letters and midterm exams.
Nothing in language could bribe a smile
that was not a relic of another month
or a memory of another mouth.

We were all part of that world she made
alive with bolts and locks, suspicious smiles.
She would not be taken; and slit-eyed
watched so that the walls would not close in.

From day to day she heard out e's and r's,
presiding over vowels and consonants,
memos that parceled syntax from each hour,
mail that moved like junkers towards each slot
until there was only heel clack, echo, silence.

No one knew her room of walled in wood,
that she would steal a Remington for a face
and take a keyboard for identity,
drawing meaning from climatic change
and light in a remote cave of things.

Nor did we know her ways at five o'clock,
whether she sat cross-legged on her bed,
but when she left we knew the room had lost
a gravity . . . and punctuation marks.

No one could be expected to hold that hand
and, if he did, not understand.

A cold November, early frosts
in patches press beneath her steps
in laced boots to the usual bench.
Under the shade of ash
Burton in the distance scowls.
She would claim him.

Scowls become eyes fixed to afternoons
through conversations that repeat
and drawing room windows that widen
into banks of Nile.
With the ceremony of tea
the river always contended.

The frost narrows the panes
at Kensington Gore, filters light
on unscrolled maps by empty chairs.
Alone, Isabel Arundell knits
her atonement stitch by stitch.
Behind the bearers' steps,
he scowls at the intruding Speke
and the infinite bends of the Nile.

With a public limp, he pauses
where student and voyeur
coalesce in arching sun.
Turning with natives, limb
on limb, in weeks of tall grass
breathing weeks of flouring dust,
Nile's source and London mist away.

Taking shorter breaths in deeper frosts
he imagines in Triestrian streets
rotations of bearers rumoring
another source of the Nile, cup
in hand, able to upset
but not disturb the guests at tea.
In falling snow he suns
in entries of carousing flesh.

What doctor and priest leave
is a nave long raged through;
scoured, scarred, all pilgrimaged
into journal page; and she
settled as an alphabet, measuring penance,
burned those scrawls and sighed
as black beads of paper
lighter than imagination
flew from the flames
and scorched the night.

PORTRAIT OF A CHILD

Alone she danced and called to mind
the aloneness of the candle's dance
negotiating with the dark.

The pelican's tender step
before the flight that balances
wind and wings
measures her whirl and tip-toed song.

She became all
and all were her
as gyrations
long and taut
funneled down the pressing air
made her soft
and nestling land
into fantasies of chosen fur.

What of other children trading
scorn, shoves, and chalk —
she danced wind to their motion;
not lonely, but alone,
rehearsing for those drifting steps
in long concrete corridors
beyond mile and measurement
when we all dance
alone.

ON ROUTE 11: WAITING ON BLOOD TESTS

I knew it as Nikos, this
café where few cars stopped.
The door is boarded up,
like a house no one visits.

I lean inside the phone booth,
its glass door flapping like paper
in wind that cuts through ferns,
disturbing by the roadside

a handful of wheat tips:
their endings, pointing
through stems to thin wind
ponds, broken spurts

of air around corn stalks.
No one remains. Some put up
signs for a year or two; the
signs drop and snow brings

the roof down. In this booth,
I dial, count white cars,
waiting to discover what
my mother is silent about

as she counts the ceiling slats
and wonders whether her corpuscles
are turning like fall leaves
into an arithmetic she understands.

WHITE TAILED CAPUCHIN MONKEY IN A MONCTON WOOLWORTH'S

The lessons
the monkey stares out in his cage
drum out a dozen
texts
of Canadian history,
disgorge volumes of Canadiana
with each touching scratch
of his genitalia.

Unconcerned with his image,
the language of the national anthem,
the compulsion to build on arable land
and till unarable land,
he sits like a flag
imprisoned
in wizened ugliness.

Unable to churn himself
into a frenzy
at the prose of the *Montreal Star*,
he has abandoned us
to the settling pointlessness
of the Laurentian shield
and himself
to the bars of his cage
between the soda counter
and the shoe department —

a joke, edible at first
it seems, but more difficult
to digest than the granite
residue of dreams

and scuttled between gratitude and compassion
I question the decorum
of slipping him a banana.

FROM MARTHA'S VINEYARD

I danced in your innocence,
trembled my love away in days
when the world was our bed —
the Peugeot's back seat, an attic cot,
fields of anemone where we'd meet
and under puzzling night birds' song
tickled wet bodies, laughed,
moaned until we yawned;
               you came
to age, your hips wider with the voyage
of two children; your fullness
opened and absorbed me —

absorbs me once again as I stare
towards the sound of evening tide,
imagine you in the space beside me.
For hours I watch headlights
approach and round the bend. Emptied,
I walk into an immense cave
of night, starless, the air still,
and discover an ache that will not leave.

NANTEL

We looked around to see
what eyes were coming up the dirt road
or staring from the lake
as we dropped our clothes,
lay beside the summer cottage
in soft grass warmed by weeks of sun.

In noonday heat you reached to me.
I turned again and again and again.
Your fingers grazed my skin like wind,
conjured my flesh into yearning
to be lost in your softness forever.
I no longer remember how we rose,
but we did, and I followed
the swing of your hips to the beach,
your plunge into the lake.

The lake is waveless now.
A lone trout scoops flies, eddies
the water. The sun has dropped.
I light the Coleman lamp
against the night.

FROZEN WHITE

Have you ever noticed
on a day when ice cuts
through wind and spears
across the lake
that you don't
touch her
hand across the sheet
　　the white full
frozen and you don't
reach across two
glasses of d'Yquem,
and you don't touch
her reaching phrase
but let it drop
into the twisted pulls
of the hooked rug
and you don't even stare
at the fire
as the cold pushes out the out
side hinges and snow
barrels down the roof
　　　　　　　　　drifting up the windows

and you don't
and you don't
and you don't

THE RECONCILIATION

Much fell from us that humid evening
with the ash leaves still,
the children long asleep.
For hours we raised accusations
before each other like flawed fruit,
and finally there was nothing left—
except, that is, a night of heavy air
and refuse all packed away
from something within us
that swelled into boulders of ache.

I still don't know what you felt
across the counter, but I
wanted you to breathe babies,
to heave like ocean, so full
I could not wind my arms around it.
You wept, we touched and were in bed.
I wound around and lost
myself in you. It must have been
hours before I could
name myself or count my toes.

UNTER DER LINDE

In the diaphanous fall of your gown
your breasts firm into moonlight.
We trouble the night at arm's length.
Over glasses of wine we linger
between distance and passion, as far
from the turned down bed as walls allow.

Fragrance of lilac contains the room;
its heavy scent hangs like an amnesty,
claiming us thigh against thigh.

In the cool of the night
you curl in love against me
like a morning flower
before the first light.

CONCEPTION

It was under a full moon
that you stepped through clothes
into a nakedness that encircled
my legs and lovemaking.
I longed to sway
with full tasseled stalks
in the keeping of the corn god

but stiffened
into a moonlight that covered you.

Schools of salmon slanted through my mind
against the current, leaping waterfalls
dropping their eggs and life
chunk by chunk.
Through moans I plunged through
your softness into softness
and in exhaustion turned
into a field of falling stars.

THE ANNOUNCEMENT

You were at the door with the news
of a life inside and we wept
that April day, the jonquils blooming
late against the wire fence.
We turned the afternoon into a bed,
measured the moving sun with mouths.

We woke in soft rain under street light,
had a sandwich and milk, and slept
in the hood of each other's arms.

I watched your landscape change
my worship growing
on your growing world

and the grass stayed green that year
right through August.

THE SKATERS

Extending hands, we shape the ice in games
by poles of light that sluice upon the pond.
Through pines the moon had shown; now slipped beyond
where skaters cannot see or skate their names.
Now only blackness, such a blackness now
as hides all sight of trees, stiff reeds that sprout
by ice we marked gliding deft figures out
from side to side, and in a truce (although
we scarcely see beneath our knees) blow
a hot skater's breath that leaves no trace
as we slice wider rings and wider race
leaning from the edge where dark shapes grow,
tilting parallel, holding tight,
our arms a skipping rope for leaps of night.

MOLIVOS: PERSPECTIVE

It is a place of sheer
ups and downs
the rise of Nikos'

bread, the fall
of wrappers
and football

shoes and hooves
sound on descent

the torrent of anemones
swished beneath the bray

of donkeys, the downhill
slope of stone to olive

groves and almond trees
dropping fruit in the wind

and "Nikolaki, ella"
tumbles from Anthi's mouth

like a sponge ball
all
   the way
      to the sea.

THE WAY WE SANG

WHITE WATER

The oars pitch
fork spray rise by
the raft's sudden
drop into
       through crushing
tunnels
     of water over
stone scrape. The white
hangs in
moments
(you
can count
if you count
fast)
    and drops
into wash
that barrels around
you barreling
through and you
tunnel mole down once
more before
you squirt
through like foam
pausing
under sun

IN A JUNGLE OF WORDS

the poet
a bird on trees
picks
by hop on hop
all insect crawl
turns
bugs into songs
of the branch

He keeps it clean

IN PRAISE OF DUCKS

Children and the aged meet
at water's edge and bend
to scatter crusts of bread
to the onrush of webbed feet.

They flap into emerging noise,
settle into martial strut.
As they move from crust to crust,
the ceremony attaches me:

Aspiring corporators come
in adoration of the dumb,
and waddling typists offer snacks
along with parenthetic quacks.

Even Ping has learned the law:
the birch for the last in line,
for the dreamer by shore or in hall
in the sprint for peanut shells.

All finally trained to come
in column to the calling hand.
They nod in committee, quack an amen
and we understand the hum

around the frenetic procession:
the spirited acquiescence, the equivocal ahem;
all huffing and puffing from promotion to promotion
for a gold inscribed ballpoint pen.

With a flutter of wings they graze the night,
leave us strutting pair by pair,
glazing the water with their wake,
bending the air in cadenced flight.

That forest of feathers we knew at noon
as comic joy, homespun surprise
becomes a splendor that removes
beyond all witnessing, all eyes.

Envoi
And yet if Robbe began to fuss
that humans strut apart from ducks,
we would argue that in fact
we know humans by their quack.

PROCESS

In spring my heroes flew
across the comic strips
with blue hair into night;
pages flipped by
my fingers and my doubts.

Spells of color,
blurs of wind,
talons of mountains
redeemed a week

of settled hours.
The rain stretches out in the gutter,
crushes the trapped leaf,
takes the window for
a blackboard.
I watch.

Winters
I scratch my toes.

AN ARTIST WITH SEVEN FINGERS

can
do many things : he
can
raise stone to
lift the firmament
        and juggle plums three
or four
at a time, he can
run one
finger round
a ripe fig
and stop if
it bleeds white
at the top,
            he can
tend his peas
by rows and
when the weather
turns cold
            cancel
all deals by fingertip
on his vaporized windshield
and stiffen one full
length to point and set
things straight
and if
not give

two fingers
to the world.

THE ONE SLOPE

A slope, really
a hillock that grazed
my eye as a boy up
to a nippled top,
that noiseless bell
touched by no wind,
and I whistled at it,
uncoupled as it stood
out there alone
over untended rows,
a duck no one would waddle with,
and I made circles of footprints
for mooncandles, the witch
grass patches spiking
like prayer pitched
from a breaking voice
and I teased them along like a boy
poking a frog, toeing
them over, and I teased them again
and they leaned
to me, I felt them lean,
until I knew the slope
as altar parts
I remembered
when I paused again

worshipping you in my own way,
my hand multiplying in its vagrancy
through rooms we root in; aloes
arbor us beyond urns from an eye beam and
we reach to childhood beyond albums
and disabled toys. We turn
and breathe in planthood,
I tongue by a lip, a hand
brushes a thigh. I understand

my turn of head that breathes
against your breast, bed
becomes breath becomes
an altar for my hand
my voice sounding words
to bell a hill, a traveller,
a mouth — it can
I can
I can till
the rows and ring
I can, can and I rang
the bell home.

SIGNAL
EDITIONS